I0200759

Learn This
And
You'll Never Be The
Same

BY
JUSTIN PERRY

Copyright © 2016 YouAreCreators Inc

All rights reserved. This book or any portion thereof may not be reproduced or used in any manner whatsoever without the express written permission of the publisher except for the use of brief quotations in a book review or for social media.

YouAreCreators

P.O. Box 756

Tinley Park, IL 60477

Message from the author

This is Justin from YouAreCreators (The Largest Self-Help YouTube Channel.) This is just one of the books in YouAreCreators "Quick Fix Collection".This short book contains information that I've personally learned and has afforded me everything that I've always wanted. The material in this book has brought me understanding, happiness, prosperity, fulfilment and peace of mind. This book contains no chapters, no fluff, and extra wording; just timeless knowledge. As with all my other books, this book gets straight into the 'juice'. I guarantee you-- if you learn this, you will never be the same. Let's get started...

Everything in the universe operates on a set of universal laws or principles. These laws can't be broken and they're always in effect no matter where you are. Some of these laws are physical, while others are quantum or spiritual laws that involve intangible properties. The more scientists study the world on a quantum level, the more they are convinced of intelligent design. Albert Einstein once said, "Every one who is seriously involved in the pursuit of science becomes convinced that a spirit is manifest in the laws of the Universe".

The spiritual laws are just as reliable as the physical laws and they ALSO affect every aspect of life on earth.

Ancient Mystics and Philosophers have known and taught these spiritual laws for thousands of years, but the majority of people are still uninformed.

I am going to teach you how to use only one of these spiritual laws in order to create and shape your personal world. What I'm about to teach you has the potential to change your life. If you can master this one principle, you can literally manifest anything in your life. This information is so simple and so easy to use that most adults will be turned off by its simplicity. For some odd reason, humans will value anything complicated and totally disregard anything made simple. Author & speaker, William Golding once said, "The greatest ideas are the simplest", and that's so true.

There are many universal laws, but the one I will be talking about is the "Law of reaping and sowing". This universal law states, "Whatever you plant in your mind, you will eventually manifest in the outside world. It's just like planting a apple seed, you first gather rich fertile soil, then you choose which apple seed you would like to plant, after that, you give it ample amounts of water and sunlight. Lastly, when the time is right and the season is set, that seed has to sprout into a mighty apple tree. The Same goes with your life. Except the soil is your mind, the seeds are your thoughts, the water is your actions and the sun is your feelings.

One thing I can guarantee, if you plant any idea in your mind, FEEL as if it's already yours and work steadying toward it, it has to manifest. It has no choice because it's law.

You might say, "Justin if that's the case, then why is it that most people don't get what they want in life?" It's simple, most people don't get what they want because they are trained to focus and think about the things they DON'T want.

You might have heard the expression, "energy flows where attention goes". Everything is energy and all energy attracts similar energy. You can't put out negative energy and expect positive results and you can't plant apple seeds expecting oranges. Likewise, you can't dwell on failure and produce a successful result. If you are constantly thinking about the things you don't want or the things you fear, you are planting that seed and based on the universal law of reaping and sowing, it will germinate...

The mind, or human consciousness seems to be literally connected to the fabric of reality. Think about something long and strong enough and it has no choice but to eventually appear. Quantum physics gives credence to this idea. Time and time again the double slit experiment has proved that a conscious observer is literally creating reality.

There are six words that I want you to memorize and stamp on your heart. These words will remind you to straighten up and think right. Think over these words anytime you get off track.

These words are: "You become what you think about." The reason why I am confident in telling you this is because this information completely transformed my life. Someone sat me down and told me the exact words I'm telling you.

When I realized that my mind was a garden, I began to plant only the things that I wanted. I was informed that the most important thing was that I knew exactly what I wanted. So, I began to write down all the things I desired. One by one I began to imagine my dream life. I wrote down exactly what I wanted in crystal-clear detail. Mind you, when I first set out to create this list **I had nothing**. I was living in a two bedroom 1 bath apartment with my wife and two children surrounded by debt and late bills. I was working a job that I hated serving tables at a restaurant, but I knew if I planted my goals successfully they would have to manifest.

So, every day I would look at my goals list and visualize my life going according to that list. I would say affirmations that complimented each goal, I drummed each idea into my head and I would imagine what it would feel like to have each goal accomplished. I visualized my goals so much that at times it was hard to tell what was real and what was imaginary. I lived into my imagination.

My mindset changed and before I knew it, things started happening around me. I started attracting the people, opportunities and ideas that helped me accomplish the goals that I set out.

Here is the actual list of my
goals……..

Goals for 2013

1. Get a house 4bedroom/3bath
   w/Basement
2. Get laser Eye Surgery
3. Get patent for sleeptight
4. Get black camaro
5. Reach 100,000 subscribers
6. Have my own positive television
   show/network.
7. Get 300i citycom scooter
8. Get motorcycle license
9. Make $100,000
10. Save $50,000 cash
11. Get app made for
    "YouAreCreators"

...and here are the things I manifested.

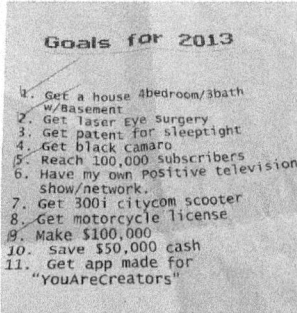

Goals for 2013

1. Get a house 4bedroom/3bath w/Basement
2. Get laser eye surgery
3. Get patent for sleeptight
4. Get black camaro
5. Reach 100,000 subscribers
6. Have my own positive television show/network.
7. Get 300i citycom scooter
8. Get motorcycle license
9. Make $100,000
10. Save $50,000 cash
11. Get app made for "YouAreCreators"

You Tube   YouAreCreators

CONGRATULATIONS
For Surpassing
100,000 Subscribers

Some of these goals took 2 months to manifest,while others took 2 years. One thing that we have to remember is that things manifest in Divine timing. There are different seasons and cycles to life. There is a season for sowing and there is a season for reaping, you can not rush the process. What I discovered was that the process helps you to develop the skills that will help you to manifest your future goals. You actually evolve as a person while going through the process. You're pushed to do things that you never thought you could do. Once your goals get embedded into your subconscious mind, you feel almost compelled to take action. Thought always precedes action.

Since your mind is a garden, weeds tend to sprout up from time to time. The weeds are your negative thoughts-- thoughts of failure and doubt. Coincidently, unlike your apple trees, weeds sprout up automatically. Since we live in a world that is obsessed with drama and negative energy, we tend to subconsciously pick up on these negative vibrations. So, every morning tend to your garden. Pluck up any thoughts that don't serve you, find the weeds and dig them up from the root. Remember, a successful gardener always cultivates their land. Cultivate your mind for success, happiness, prosperity, kindness, forgiveness, love, opulence, understanding, gratitude, and abundance. As you do this, you'll notice how those seeds sprout and manifest in your life. Life is a constant reaping and sowing, what you give, you receive. The energy you put out is what you get back and how you treat others is how you'll eventually be treated. What you say about others will be said about you. As Florence Scovel Shinn would say, "The game of life is the game of boomerangs. Our thoughts, deeds and words return to us sooner or later with astounding accuracy." If you master this single law, you will be able to create happiness in all areas of your life. One thing that you have to remember is your thoughts are seeds and your mind is fertile land. The mind doesn't care what you plant in it, it will always yield results. You can plant vegetables or your can plant weeds, you can plant wealth, or you can plant poverty. You can plant misery or you can plant happiness.

It's all up to you, because you are always reaping what you sow.

This is Justin from YouAreCreators and we support your dreams.

www.ingramcontent.com/pod-product-compliance
Lightning Source LLC
Chambersburg PA
CBHW071942020426
42331CB00010B/2989